Butterflies!

Written by Darlene Freeman
Illustrated by Mike Maydak

Text reviewed by Louis Sorkin,
Department of Entomology, American Museum of Natural History

HILLSDALE PUBLIC LIBRARY
HILLSDALE, NEW JERSEY

© 1999 McClanahan Book Company, Inc.
All rights reserved.
Published by McClanahan Book Company, Inc.
23 West 26th Street, New York, NY 10010
ISBN: 0-7681-0131-X
Printed in the U.S.A.
10 9 8 7 6 5

In the spring, crawling caterpillars appear, munching on plants. Soon butterflies fill the air, flitting from flower to flower. Have you ever wondered where all those hungry caterpillars and beautiful butterflies come from?

Turn the page to find out!

Life Cycle of a Butterfly

One of the most amazing transformations in nature happens as a butterfly grows. It completely changes the way it looks! This change is called **metamorphosis** (met-uh-MOR-foh-sis). This cycle has four steps.

Gulf Fritillary egg

Chalcedon Checkerspot eggs

European Cabbage White eggs

1. Eggs

A butterfly begins its life as an egg. Most female butterflies lay their eggs on the kinds of plants their caterpillars will want to eat. Some butterfly eggs hatch in a few days. Others hatch in a few months.

2. The Caterpillar

When the butterfly **larva** (LAR-vah), better known as a caterpillar, hatches from the egg, it has an ENORMOUS appetite. It usually begins by eating its own eggshell! Then, with its oversized jaws, called **mandibles**, it begins to eat plants.

Gulf Fritillary hatching from egg

mandibles

Gulf Fritillary larva

molting

The caterpillar eats . . . and eats . . . and *EATS*! It finally gets too big for its own skin! When this happens, the old skin splits open and the caterpillar crawls out of it wearing a new skin. This is called **molting**.

3. The Pupa

The caterpillar spins silk and then attaches itself to a twig.

The caterpillar molts. It emerges as a prepupa.

When a caterpillar reaches full size, it molts to reveal a soft new body called a prepupa. Its soft, tender body slowly hardens to form a **chrysalis** (KRIS-uh-lis).

Its soft body becomes a chrysalis.

The butterfly is in its third stage of metamorphosis, the pupa.

Inside this hard shell, the insect, now called a **pupa**, changes into an adult butterfly. This transformation can take a few days for some kinds of butterflies or up to a year for others.

4. The Adult

When the adult butterfly is fully formed, the chrysalis cracks open. The butterfly frees itself from the hard shell.

Metamorphosis

- Hatches from an egg
- Molts as the caterpillar grows
- Forms a chrysalis in the pupa stage
- Emerges from chrysalis as an adult

Monarch

At first, its wings are soft and crumpled. The butterfly pumps blood into its wings so that they will spread and harden. In an hour or two, it is ready to fly!

Butterfly Body Parts

Like all insects, butterflies have six legs and three main body parts: a **head**, a **thorax**, and an **abdomen**.

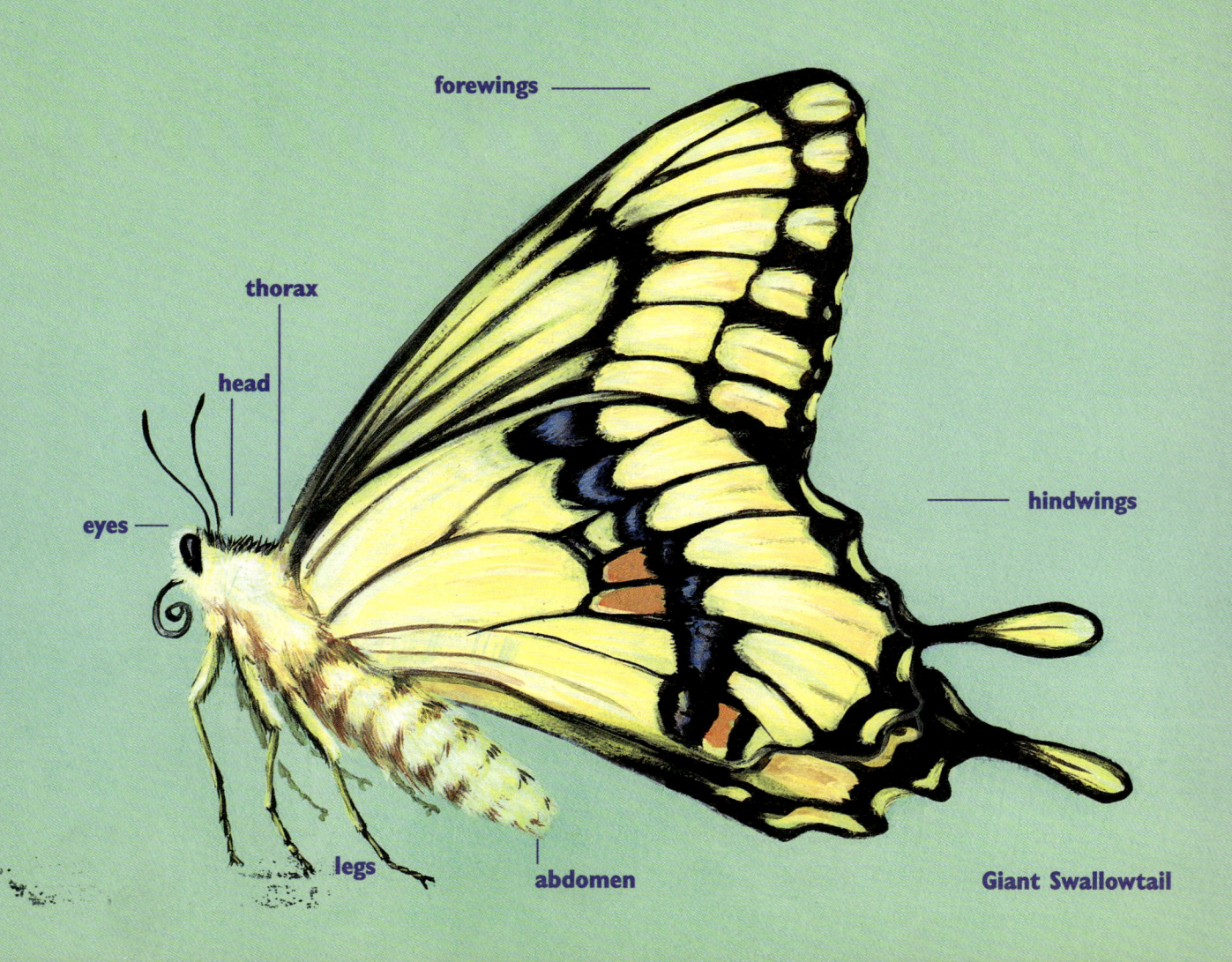

forewings

thorax

head

eyes

hindwings

legs

abdomen

Giant Swallowtail

antennae

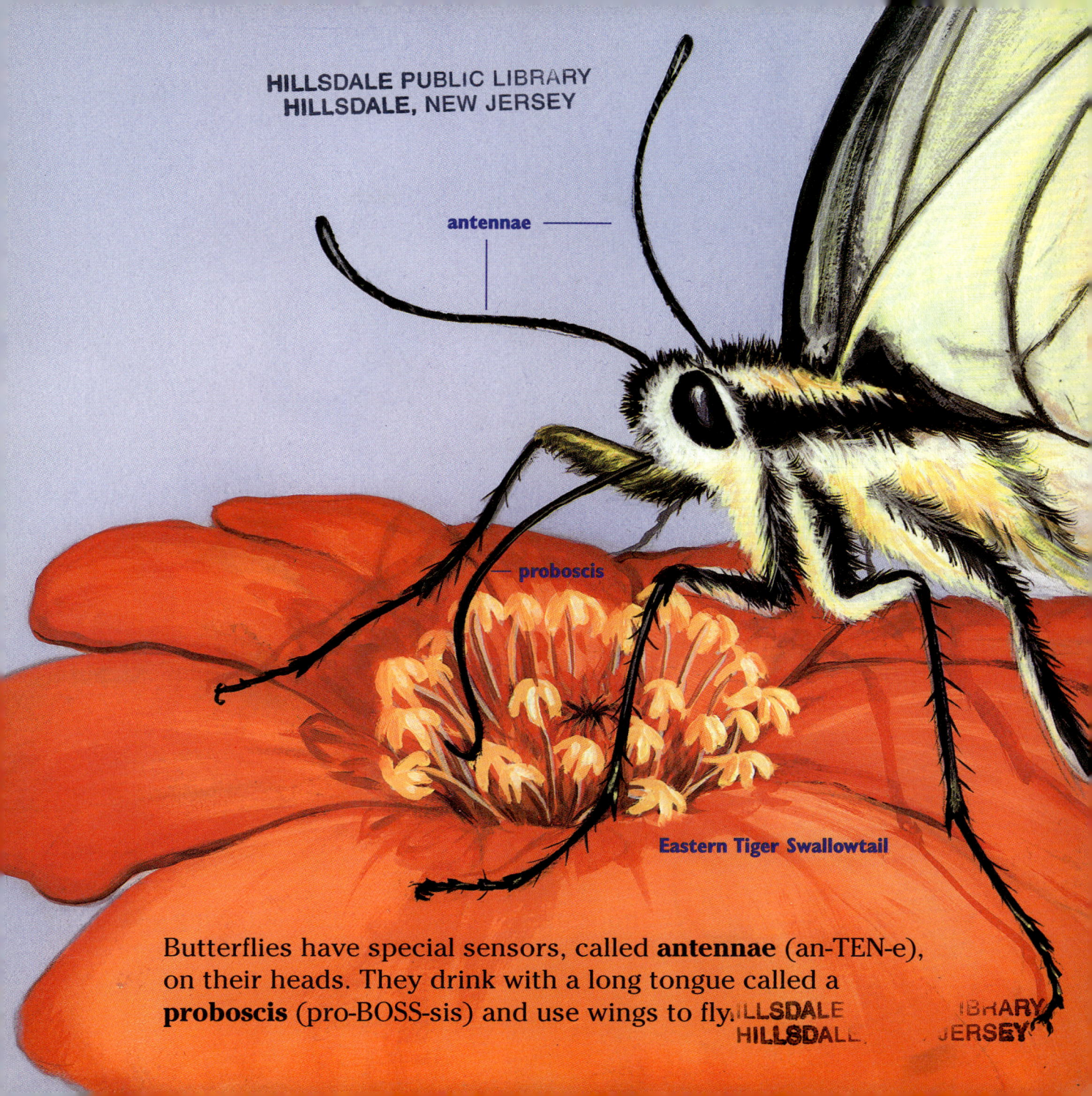

proboscis

Eastern Tiger Swallowtail

Butterflies have special sensors, called **antennae** (an-TEN-e), on their heads. They drink with a long tongue called a **proboscis** (pro-BOSS-sis) and use wings to fly.

Butterfly Life

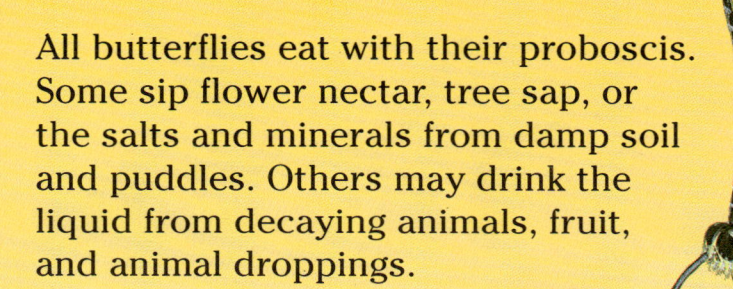

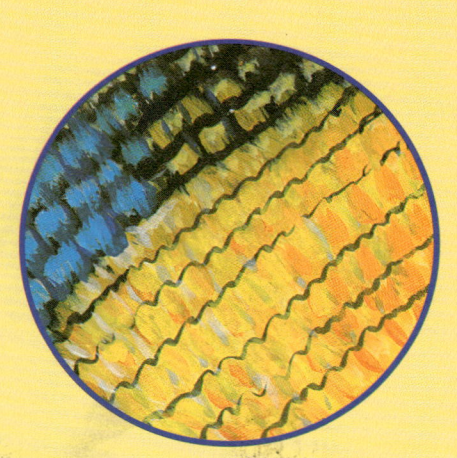

All butterflies eat with their proboscis. Some sip flower nectar, tree sap, or the salts and minerals from damp soil and puddles. Others may drink the liquid from decaying animals, fruit, and animal droppings.

Clearwing

Gray Hairstreak

Thousands of tiny scales on each wing give a butterfly its colors. Butterflies are a type of insect called **Lepidoptera** (lep-eh-DOP-terah), which means "scaly wings"!

Butterflies find food and locate a mate with their eyes, "smell" and sense vibrations with their antennae, and taste with their front feet!

Postman Butterfly

Peacock Butterflies

During the winter some butterflies hibernate in caves, under leaves, inside houses, and in other safe places.

A Long Journey

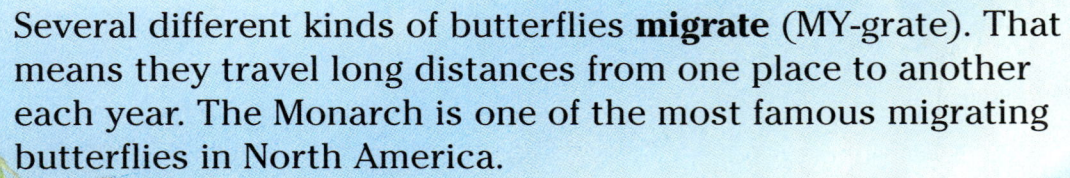

Several different kinds of butterflies **migrate** (MY-grate). That means they travel long distances from one place to another each year. The Monarch is one of the most famous migrating butterflies in North America.

Monarch

Fact

- Monarchs migrate thousands of miles.

Summer
Fall/Winter

In the fall when the weather gets cold, swarms of Monarch butterflies migrate from as far north as Canada to sunny California and Mexico. In the spring, they lay their eggs which hatch. The new butterflies fly back north—the round-trip is almost 4,000 miles (6,436 km) long. Those Monarchs lay more eggs that hatch and begin the journey south again!

Masters of Disguise

Butterflies need to protect themselves from birds, lizards, monkeys, spiders, and other predators. Some butterflies have colors and patterns on their wings that help them stay hidden.

They can appear to be part of a rock, a leaf, a tree, a flower, or something else in their environment. This is called **camouflage** (KA-ma-flahj).

Can you find the three butterflies hidden on this page?

Other Defenses

Butterflies can defend themselves in many other ways.

Viceroy, a mimic

Monarch

Some butterflies, such as the Monarch, taste bad. Other butterflies, called **mimics**, just happen to look like them. Predators leave them both alone rather than eat the wrong one!

female

male

In some butterfly families, the males are more colorful than the females. Predators see and eat more of the males, so more females survive to lay eggs!

Defenses
- Camouflage
- Bad taste and smell
- Mimicry
- Wing spots
- Flashy colors

Owl Butterfly

Wing spots that look like eyes or flashy coloring can startle predators and give the butterfly a chance to escape.

Old World Swallowtail caterpillar

Some caterpillars use unpleasant odors to drive predators away.

Bet you didn't know...

Overall, the Queen Alexandria Birdwing is the biggest butterfly in the world. It's twice as big as this picture!

The Western Pygmy Blue is one of the smallest butterflies. Its wings are only 3/8 inch (1 cm) across. This picture is twice as big as a real Western Pygmy Blue!

Some caterpillars have eyespots and other markings that make them look like a little snake.

Spicebush Swallowtail

The Question Mark is a curious little butterfly that has markings on its wings that look like question marks.

Some swallowtail caterpillars make tents out of leaves for shelter.

Butterflies Everywhere!

Purplish Copper

Monarch

Common Swallowtail

Regal Fritillary

Cabbage White

Common Sulfer

There are over 10,000 named species of butterflies in the world—and many more left to be discovered! You would have to find 10 different species a day for three years to come close to seeing them all. Better start looking now!